Farm Animals

Ducks

by Betsy Rathburn

BELLWETHER MEDIA
MINNEAPOLIS, MN

Blastoff! Beginners are developed by literacy experts and educators to meet the needs of early readers. These engaging informational texts support young children as they begin reading about their world. Through simple language and high frequency words paired with crisp, colorful photos, Blastoff! Beginners launch young readers into the universe of independent reading.

Sight Words in This Book

and	eat	look	them
are	get	many	they
at	have	on	this
be	help	that	to
by	it	the	up
can	like	their	water

This edition first published in 2024 by Bellwether Media, Inc.

No part of this publication may be reproduced in whole or in part without written permission of the publisher. For information regarding permission, write to Bellwether Media, Inc., Attention: Permissions Department, 6012 Blue Circle Drive, Minnetonka, MN 55343.

Library of Congress Cataloging-in-Publication Data

Names: Rathburn, Betsy, author.
Title: Ducks / by Betsy Rathburn.
Description: Minneapolis, MN : Bellwether Media, 2024. | Series: Blastoff! Beginners: Farm Animals | Includes bibliographical references and index. | Audience: Ages 4-7 | Audience: Grades K-1
Identifiers: LCCN 2023039746 (print) | LCCN 2023039747 (ebook) | ISBN 9798886877601 (library binding) | ISBN 9798886879483 (paperback) | ISBN 9798886878547 (ebook)
Subjects: LCSH: Ducks--Juvenile literature. | Farm life--Juvenile literature.
Classification: LCC QL696.A52 R3753 2024 (print) | LCC QL696.A52 (ebook) | DDC 598.4/1--dc23 eng/20230831
LC record available at https://lccn.loc.gov/2023039746
LC ebook record available at https://lccn.loc.gov/2023039747

Text copyright © 2024 by Bellwether Media, Inc. BLASTOFF! BEGINNERS and associated logos are trademarks and/or registered trademarks of Bellwether Media, Inc.

Editor: Elizabeth Neuenfeldt   Designer: Laura Sowers

Printed in the United States of America, North Mankato, MN.

Table of Contents

Ducks Swim!	4
What Are Ducks?	6
Life on the Farm	12
Duck Facts	22
Glossary	23
To Learn More	24
Index	24

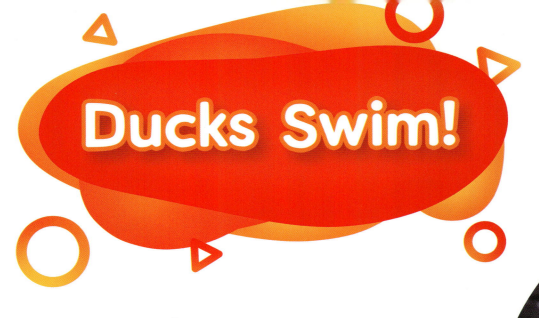

Ducks Swim!

Look at that pond. Those ducks like to swim!

pond

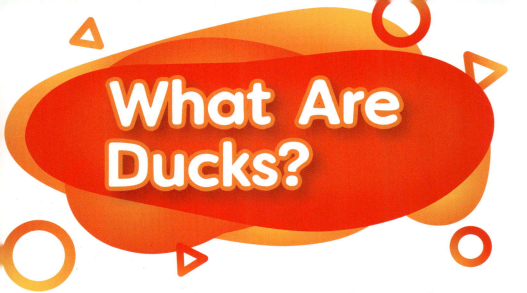

What Are Ducks?

Ducks are birds. They have **feathers**. They can be many colors!

feathers

They have **webbed feet**.
Their feet help them swim.

webbed feet

They have **bills**.
Bills help ducks
pick up food.

bill

Life on the Farm

Ducks live on farms. They stay by ponds.

farm

13

They dip their heads underwater. They eat bugs and plants. Yum!

Farmers feed them **grains**.

bugs

grains

plants

grains

Female ducks lay eggs. Farmers get the eggs.

eggs

This duck found water.
It likes to splash.
Quack!

Duck Facts

Parts of a Duck

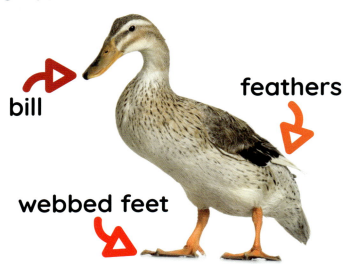

bill

feathers

webbed feet

Life on the Farm

swim   eat   lay eggs

Glossary

the mouths of birds

soft coverings on ducks

seeds of plants

feet with thin skin that connects the toes

To Learn More

ON THE WEB

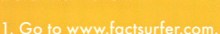

Factsurfer.com gives you a safe, fun way to find more information.

1. Go to www.factsurfer.com.
2. Enter "ducks" into the search box and click 🔍.
3. Select your book cover to see a list of related content.

Index

bills, 10
birds, 6
bugs, 14, 16
colors, 6
eat, 14
eggs, 18
farmers, 16, 18
farms, 12
feathers, 6
females, 18
food, 10, 14, 16, 17
grains, 16, 17
heads, 14
plants, 14, 17
pond, 4, 5, 12
quack, 20
splash, 20
swim, 4, 8
water, 14, 20
webbed feet, 8

The images in this book are reproduced through the courtesy of: bazlifoto, cover; natthawut ngoensanthia, p. 3; Aleksandr Kondratov, pp. 4-5; DenisNata, pp. 6, 10; Eric Isselee, pp. 7, 22; Andi Edwards, pp. 8, 20-21; Andy119, pp. 8-9; Andi111, pp. 10-11, 23 (bills); MaxyM, p. 12; Kiki vera yasmina, pp. 12-13; nameinfame, pp. 14-15; srimapan, pp. 16-17; Joseph Skompski, p. 16 (bugs); Jovana Pantovic, p. 17 (plants); Robert J. Bradshaw, p. 17 (grains); kungfu01, p. 18; yaibuabann, pp. 18-19; kzww, p. 22 (swim); Margarita Kosior, p. 22 (eat); John And Penny, p. 22 (lay eggs); Olhastock, p. 23 (feathers); Shamils, p. 23 (grains); Chrispo, p. 23 (webbed feet).